Y

CON

CAPRICORN 2023 PERSONAL HOROSCOPE

Monthly Astrological Prediction Forecast Readings of Every Zodiac Astrology Sun Star Signs- Love, Romance, Money, Finances, Career, Health, Travel, Spirituality.

Iris Quinn

Alpha Zuriel Publishing

Your Complete Capricorn 2023 Personal Horoscope/ Iris Quinn. -- 1st ed.

We are born at a specific time and place, and, like vintage years of wine, we have the characteristics of the year and season in which we are born. Astrology claims nothing more.
— CARL JUNG

CONTENTS

CHAPTER ONE

CAPRICORN

Constellation: Capricorn
Zodiac symbol: Sea Goat
Date: December 21 – January 19
Zodiac element: Earth
Zodiac quality: Cardinal
Greatest Compatibility: Cancer and Taurus
Sign ruler: Saturn
Day: Saturday
Color: Black and Brown
Birthstone: Garnet

CAPRICORN TRAITS

- Matures early.
- The responsible buddy.
- Driven by motivation
- It takes time to warm up to someone.
- Any emotion that gets in the way of accomplishment is suppressed.

PERSONALITY OF CAPRICORN

Capricorns are disciplined individuals. The wringing of hands, the continual reminders, the strict framework, the ever-increasing ambitions, the never-ending tide of self-criticism They are the epitome of perfectionists. They can become so engrossed in their own internal monologue that it becomes tough to convince them to turn away. Capricorns are frequently referred to as "workaholics."

They are really practical. They are rule-followers with a strong moral compass. It is instilled in them from an early age that their entire feeling of worth and significance is reliant on their capacity to burrow down and force their way to the finish line. This makes them achievement junkies. Their will to succeed reflects their fear of failing. Capricorns experience the most stress when they challenge their own authority. Capricorns are most steady when they are in positions of power. When they are forced to adhere to someone else's agenda, they can become a little out of control.

Capricorns are collectors of responsibilities. And they always seem to take on everything. Capricorns like to be the ones to solve all problems. Their inherent state is one of responsibility. They have a "can-do" mentality. They are both martyrs and heroes. They serve as both guardians and judges. The captains of the team. The supreme commander. The commander-in-chief. The boss. Even when they lead the charge, Capricorns can feel the most alone in the world. They want to be entirely self-sufficient and are afraid to rely on others.

WEAKNESSES OF CAPRICORN

Capricorns are not obsessed by the desire for attention, but they are not immune to it either. Simply put, they do not engage in attention-seeking conduct. They don't want to be noticed for their appearance, style, or ingenuity. They do not seek to be admired, but rather to be respected. They do not wish to be the focus of attention. Instead, they appear to be trying to prove their own abilities to themselves.

Capricorns are always competing against themselves. They do, however, seek recognition. Not adoration, but only praise. Praise is simply recognizing a job well done. A compliment is a pat on the back. This serves as validation for their general sense of ineptitude and inferiority. They plough through difficulties while wearing blinders until they achieve victory.

RELATIONSHIP COMPATIBILITY WITH CAPRICORN

Based only on their Sun signs, this is how Capricorn interacts with others. These are the compatibility interpretations for all 12 potential Capricorn combinations. This is a limited and insufficient method of determining compatibility.

However, Sun-sign compatibility remains the foundation for overall harmony in a relationship.

The general rule is that yin and yang do not get along. Yin complements yin, and yang complements yang. While yin and yang partnerships can be successful, they require more effort. Earth and water zodiac signs are both Yin. Yang is represented by the fire and air zodiac signs.

Aries and Capricorn

Capricorn and Aries have an extremely challenging relationship. Their personalities are too dissimilar to complement one another harmoniously. Aries acts on impulse without forethought, whereas Capricorn meticulously plans before taking action. Capricorn's continual criticism will not be tolerated by Aries.

Capricorn's tone is too authoritative for Aries. Capricorn, on the other hand, will have a tough time supporting Aries' style of life, which Capricorn regards as silly.

Taurus and Capricorn

Capricorn and Taurus are two earth signs that work really well together. They will enjoy this relationship because they will do it their way: step by step, planning each movement, perfecting what works, celebrating with a movie at home, and triumphantly reaching the peak. Everything is in their favor for a long-term partnership.

Gemini and Capricorn

Capricorn and Gemini were not meant to be together. Capricorns will spend their lives criticizing Gemini for its lack of concentration and for changing its mind so frequently. Capricorn's mental rigidity, on the other hand, will swiftly bore Gemini. Gemini will become impatient with the fact that it finds no way to really enjoy life with such a mate. It may work with hard work and a lot of love.

Cancer and Capricorn

Capricorn and Cancer can have a wonderful partnership. In terms of safety and material well-being, Capricorn has a lot to give Cancer. Cancer will show Capricorn that life is more than just labor and mental fields: Cancer will teach Capricorn to appreciate life in ways Capricorn has never dreamed. There are no major issues with this connection.

Leo and Capricorn

A connection between Capricorn and Leo will expose one another's selfishness. They each seek complete control over everything around them. They are both determined to be the first in the relationship. They each believe they have the finest solutions to various problems. Finally, Leo and Capricorn will simply compete and argue about who has the upper hand in the relationship.

Virgo and Capricorn

Capricorn and Virgo will make a terrific couple. Just be careful not to become stuck in a suffocating rut. Both Virgo and Capricorn struggle to actively appreciate life. They should assist one another in this regard. Everything else went swimmingly.

Libra and Capricorn

On an intellectual level, Capricorn and Libra complement each other beautifully. In that regard, they are excellent complements to one another and will make excellent companions. Capricorn, on the other hand, does not accept the ups and downs in Libra's life, which are caused by Libra's persistent hesitation over which action to take.

Scorpio and Capricorn

Capricorn and Scorpio are compatible signs. Scorpio's intuition combines with Capricorn's depth of analysis, and they will have many wonderful times learning new things about themselves and the world around them. They should be careful not to separate themselves from the rest of the world too much.

Sagittarius and Capricorn

Capricorn will be captivated by Sagittarius at the start of the relationship because of the free and happy way in which Sagittarius lives their life. Capricorn will assist Sagittarius with everyday planning and material support. However, it will take a lot of effort to keep the relationship going in the long run without harshly condemning each other's differences along the road.

Capricorn and Capricorn

Two Capricorns in a relationship will completely understand each other. The dangers are: wanting to compete for first position in the relationship, forming an extremely structured relationship, being highly critical of each other in pursuit of perfectionism, and demonstrating excessive stubbornness.

Aquarius and Capricorn

Capricorn and Aquarius will be fascinated by each other at first, but they will not find a safe refuge in their partnership. Capricorn and Aquarius have quite different personalities. They will clash if one expects the other to act in a way that is antithetical to their nature. Maybe they'll make it with a lot of love.

Pisces and Capricorn

Capricorn will provide an incredible world for Pisces since Capricorn will take care of fixing any difficulties, anticipating potential conflicts, and maintaining the home from the start. Pisces will believe that it has discovered the love of its life and will lavishly pamper and caress Capricorn. Pisces, on the other hand, must learn to bear Capricorn's regular bouts of emotional coldness.

LOVE AND PASSION

When it comes to relationships, some Capricorns are fairly traditional. Before asking someone out, these people prefer to be professionally acquainted. If they really like someone, they will ask them to a nice restaurant for supper to create the best impression.

In general, they don't like to get sexually involved unless they have a relationship that is fairly stable and safe. Some Capricorns are really rigid about this. They can only shed their inhibitions with a gentle and delicate companion and become passionate and impulsive lovers when they trust the other person.

Capricorns are prone to becoming petty and even cruel. Those who enjoy an active social life may struggle to adjust to Capricorn's seriousness. They are, on the other hand, exceedingly devoted and consistent, and are not prone to extramarital affairs. They are highly caring when they feel loved.

MARRIAGE

Capricorns take marriage obligations very seriously. They feel that marriage is sacred. When they commit, they do so fully aware that they intend for it to be permanent.

Because Capricorns are orderly, household tasks should be kept to a minimum. They always have money set aside for emergencies. In general, a Capricorn's spouse will not have to worry about money.

A Capricorn's profession might be a source of contention because they can occasionally prioritize it over their personal life. They are so focused on their work in order to be successful that they sometimes neglect their spouse and children. They must make a sincere attempt to balance work, marriage, and family.

Capricorn women manage to balance the demands of their work, children, and spouse because of their maternal instinct. In their more traditional roles, Capricorn males may tend to compartmentalize work, marriage, and family. They are compassionate and caring at home when the timing is right.

CHAPTER TWO

CAPRICORN 2023 HOROSCOPE

Overview Capricorn 2023

Jupiter, the planet of fortune and knowledge, will spend the first quarter of this year in Capricorn's 4th house. Then it moves to the 5th house of Taurus in May. So, at the start of the year, Capricorns will have a happy home life, do well in real estate deals, and gain materially. With the move to the 5th, love, luck, and children become more important. Saturn, the planet of discipline, moves through Aquarius, which is your second house. This affects your finances. Then, in March 2023, it moves to your third house of Pisces, which affects how you get along with your siblings and travel.

Uranus will transit through the 5th house of the horoscope for Capricorns. Neptune moves through your 3rd house of Pisces at the beginning of the year, and Pluto moves through your Ascendant. In May and June 2023, Pluto will move to your 2nd house of Aquarius. Capricorns' lives are definitely affected by these planetary movements throughout the year.

This year, you will take care of your love life and marriage. Capricorns will have a good year in the long run. On your part, you wouldn't have to do much. A partner or spouse would be drawn to you this time and become your loving friend. Venus makes it easier to get along with your partner for the year. Your love life would be peaceful and happy.

This year, Capricorns will have average luck in their careers. As the year starts, you will have good work relationships with your peers and the people in charge. This is because of Jupiter's good qualities. This is a good time for Capricorns to get ahead in their careers. Saturn, however, may provide some challenges to your career.

Capricorns will have a year of good health and happiness in 2023, thanks to the influence of the planets. As a result of achieving both personal and professional success, you'll feel better about yourself, leading to more excellent health. When it comes to health care decisions, trust your intuition. Do not ignore any indications of illness that raise a red flag.

The problem may be avoided if you receive prompt medical attention and use effective preventative measures. Also, relax and recharge your batteries from time to time.

In 2023, Capricorns would do well with their money. At the beginning of the year, Jupiter will be in your 11th house of Scorpio, which is a good time. Money would come in well, and you'd be able to pay off loans, debts, and overdue bills. Capricorns, however, may have to make financial sacrifices this year due to financial obligations related to their families. With Jupiter moving through the 4th house of Aries, you would get a lot of real estate and nice cars. Landed property deals could be good for you in the year's first three months. This year, money would also come from a legacy or an inheritance.

With Jupiter in the fourth house of Aries at the beginning of the year, Capricorns may feel pressure from their families. When it passes, things will get better. Both Saturn and Jupiter make sure that your family life is going well. There would be good relationships at home, partners would be loyal, and you would be more devoted to your family than you usually are, which is not like you. Throughout the year, you would have many wonderful times with your family.

Regarding travel, the Capricorns will have a pretty good year. As the new year begins, Jupiter favors some short trips that aren't too far away because of work. After the transit of Jupiter in May 2023, you'll be able to take long trips for fun and pleasure. Some of you may be going home for the first time in a long time. Traveling this year, Capricorns should exercise extreme caution when it comes to their wealth and health since problems and mishaps are almost inevitable for those born under the sign.

The year 2023 would be a good time for you to do religious ceremonies. As Jupiter moves through your 9th house, you will become more interested in religious acts during this time. Your faith and sense of belief would reach a whole new level. Pilgrimages are likely if you want the same thing in recent years. You would also do pujas for the planets and take steps to fix any bad doshas. Do social and charity work that will bring you many blessings throughout the year.

Be realistic about your goals for the year and confident you will achieve them. Keep a positive outlook and trust your intuition even when things look bleak. Use your position to help improve society and discover ways to live that benefit everyone. You'll reach new heights if you're honest, loyal, and disciplined in your job. You would face problems, so be firm and steady and stick to your policies no matter what. Keep dreaming big because you have a lot to do this year.

January 2023

Horoscope

You feel tight at the start of this year. You are burning with the need to reach your goals or to be on your own. You can't wait any longer. So, people don't take you too seriously. You are ready to fight the first challenge from the outside.

The full moon makes you irritable, so watch how you act around the 6th. But this state of being is not a small thing. Do you have a plan or project that you are working on? Even though Jupiter is in a different sign from yours, it is still possible for Jupiter to give you some opportunities. The important thing is whether or not you can trust them. Dare to put your cards on the table to do this. It will definitely make things more complicated, but you'll know if you have to deal with it or not.

Love

You're angry, which doesn't help with things that have to do with your heart. If you aren't careful, you'll have a rough time on all fronts, making things hard for you. You might feel like time is moving slowly. Understanding comes back on the 28th.

When the moon is full, you must say what you think. In return, your partner may feel too much stress from all the negativity. The amount of talking is kept to a strict minimum. Venus helps you be forgiven after the 28th.

Single Capricorns, Things keep coming up until the 4th, making things more complicated. Get to know your loves better to keep them from going in the wrong direction. With Venus in Pisces, all the lights will be green starting on the 28th.

Career

Even though you try hard, you just can't get yourself together until the 13th. When you think you have everything in order, something unexpected comes up. After this challenging time, something better starts to happen. You are all over the place. There are proposals for you. You have to wait and see if they can be trusted or not. Take your time to think about it, even if others want you to hurry up and make a decision.

The way the stars are aligned in front of you doesn't look good for your career. There would be a lot of short trips that wouldn't bring the expected benefits. On the other hand, a trip to the North would be helpful. During this time, it's not likely that people you know will be able to help you much.

So, it would be a good idea to trust in your ability to solve problems. But there are reasons to think that the working conditions and atmosphere would stay pretty good. This would be a big reason to be happy. Overall, it was a month when you had to be careful with several sensitive matters.

Finance

Saturn watches over this area in terms of money. It doesn't make you make sacrifices, but it does keep you from wasting money, which isn't so bad.

Even though you'll be hanging out with many smart and spiritually gifted people this month, it won't improve your finances. There is a good chance that you would have to work hard to reach your goals, and even then, you might not get very far.

The climate would also not be suitable for making investments or starting up new businesses. They might get stuck. Also, banks or other financial institutions would unlikely approve any pending loan applications or requests for new advances. Also, people who do business overseas would probably have to deal with adversity.

Health

A great month when the stars are aligned to give
you good health, and you don't have to do much but sit
back and enjoy it. Your body would get the most out of
what you eat, and your health would shine as a result.

Not only would you be very busy and full of energy
during the month, but you would also keep your mind
and body in good shape. There are some reasons to be
careful about boils that might make you uncomfortable
for a short time. With quick medicine, you don't have
to worry about anything.

Travel

Since this part of the astrological forecast isn't very
good, you wouldn't gain much from travelling this
month. But there are some people who have to travel
to keep their jobs or businesses going. The answer
would be to find a middle ground where you cut your
losses and do as much as possible on your travel
situation.

Artists, singers, dancers, and others like them
wouldn't get the usual benefits from travel. Those who
go abroad to study at a college or university may face
different problems. Business trips to other countries

would not be very productive either. North is the best direction to go.

Insight from the stars

The full moon establishes this month's mood on the 6th. Think about the pros and cons of your thoughts, decisions, and actions before you act quickly. If everyone in your family gets along, you will have a happy home life.

February 2023

Horoscope

The energies of Capricorn, Taurus, and Pisces put you in a comfortable place where you can show off your best qualities. Your mood is less defensive. So, you are easier to reach. You are interested in what other people have to say. You always show empathy in how you say what you think. So, the past few weeks' tensions are starting to disappear.

But the conflicts that come from Aries are still going on. The 21st, when Venus moves into this sign, confirms them. Even though it's less dangerous, it makes you feel uncomfortable. You want to take charge, but something keeps you from doing so. It won't help to yell in every direction. Use this time of peace to think about what you want to accomplish.

Love

The energy of the friendly signs makes you more available to your loved ones and helps them find their way. Use it to fix relationships that have been hurt by conflict until the 20th. Don't make the same mistakes again if you want peace to last after the 21st.

Venus in Pisces brings back communication with your partner. You are willing to do what they want. Between the two of you, things are easy. But watch out for the dissonances that Venus in Aries still gives you.

For single Capricorns, Venus in Pisces makes it easier for you to connect with someone special. Your charm stirs up sincere feelings. At the end of the month, instead of blocking this special person's ideas, accept them.

Career

You are working hard in this sector. To achieve your goals, you don't count the hours. The only problem with this helpful program is that you can get stressed out. In these situations, your mood can change quickly, which can throw off your business partners. To avoid this, be kind to people who don't have as much stamina as you do. Don't rush them. Give them the time they need. If you need to, share what you know.

The combination of stars facing you doesn't look good for your career. There would be a lot of hard work, but the benefits would not match the work done. Also, travel is mentioned, but this too wouldn't live up to expectations in a meaningful way.

Connections won't help you much during this time, but some female coworkers or friends will try to promote your professional achievements. It would be better to rely mostly on your own skills and work—a month in which you would have to work very hard to keep going.

Finance

On the money side, money keeps coming in. But the delays are getting longer. Don't put yourself under pressure. Everything will turn out fine.

The stars don't seem to be in a particularly good mood this month, so you shouldn't expect anything good to happen financially. Even if you worked very hard, your current operations wouldn't give you the expected or planned results. There are also no good signs for starting a new business or expanding an existing one.

If you tried to get a loan from a bank or other financial institution, your project would probably move slowly and get in the way. There is also a chance that people who deal with parties outside your country will have a hard time and even lose money.

Health

A good month in which you will be healthy, grow and get stronger thanks to the food you eat. This means that you are in good health and your body is getting the most out of your food. Any sudden, severe illness should be taken seriously, and treatment should be started right away.

If you treat these symptoms as soon as you notice them, you can be sure that nothing serious will happen. A good month that doesn't require much attention.

Travel

The stars are not aligned in a way that makes this a good month for making money through travel. During your travels, you could get hurt or have other physical problems. You should be careful because of this.

Also, your job or business would require a certain amount of travel this month. This wouldn't work out very well, though. Even trips to the West, which is the best direction, would not help. Some of you might go on a trip abroad, which wouldn't get you anywhere and might not help you achieve your goals.

Insight from the stars

If you want peace to rule your life and your love, give your entourage time, and don't let your ambitions take over. The whole month will be full of love and romance. You and your partner will have a lot of fun. Find ways to make memories with the person you care about most.

March 2023

Horoscope

The Aries energies are still putting you under pressure. A chance or an opportunity needs to be confirmed. As a result, you feel that you need to make a decision as soon as possible. The energy in the friendly signs is there to support you. They keep you from making rash decisions.

Saturn's transfer urges you to focus on what suits you and is convenient for you beginning on the 8th. These energies relieve stress and encourage you to take your time rather than haste. They inspire you to consider your goals. Saturn establishes a buffer zone so the external agitation does not affect you as much as it used to. As a result, you develop this discernment that allows you to make the best judgments for yourself.

Love

You're becoming better and better. You gradually regain command of the situation. But the situation is still tense! Venus in Taurus, which starts on the 17th, brings you back in touch with people who share your values. Your loved ones find their way and get back to basics.

The dissonances that come from Aries spoil your mood. Your level of understanding is low, and you are irritable. Things started to get better on the 17th. From the 26th, you should be happy to go along with what your partner wants to do.

Single Capricorn, The stars make things happen that are good for your love, a chance meeting, or the start of a romance. Leave your pain alone if you want things to go well. Accept what you are given at the end of the month.

Career

Your daily growth hasn't been natural for a while now because it depends on choices that don't always make sense. But you find ways to make things work, thanks to your legendary wisdom and experience. When Saturn comes into your sign, you should feel much more relaxed and less stressed. In this situation, you can breathe and still do your job well.

But even if you worked extremely hard, you probably wouldn't get the desired results.

There would be a lot of travel, but it wouldn't go as planned, though a trip to the South might be helpful. It would be best to rely on your skills and resources as much as possible. Overall, it is a month in which you must be very careful about dealing with difficult situations.

Finance

From a financial point of view, this sector is doing great. But you could treat yourself around the 7th. If so, make a rule for yourself and stick to it.

You should do very well financially this month because the stars are aligned in your favor. People who do business with other countries or across state lines would do very well and gain a lot. You would be able to get the planned gains from your current operations during this time.

Also, this would be a good situation for people who want to grow their businesses or start new ones. Those who have loan requests pending with any bank or financial institution will be able to obtain the loans they require. It's important to remember that working with women in business or the workplace would be beneficial.

Health

A month in which you're almost certain to be in good health. People prone to long-term problems like rheumatism and too much gas in the digestive tract will feel much better. They only need to use the usual amount of care to get relief from their illnesses.

The food you eat will really feed your body and keep you in great shape. You will have above-average reproductive vitality, giving you a healthy mind and body. There are a few reasons to take a sore throat seriously if you have one. The rest should go well.

Travel

The signs from the stars make it clear that there isn't much chance of making money from traveling. People whose jobs or businesses take them around a lot will not get much out of the exercise. You wouldn't be able to make much money from your business trips. Going in the best direction, South, would not change the situation. You could worsen your problems by going on expensive trips abroad that don't accomplish your goals. This could make things much worse for you. Under these circumstances, you should keep your plans as simple as possible.

Insight from the stars

Planets in friendly signs act like a wall that keeps outside pressure away from you. Be open to new ideas, and don't be afraid to try them out. You won't be sorry about it. It's time for you to make changes that will make your life better. Make sure you don't go down a path in life that will bring you down.

April 2023

Horoscope

Pressure from Aries starts to go away, and since happiness never comes on its own, you benefit from the energies moving through Taurus. Your mood is better when Saturn is close by. This month, your ambitions still drive you, but in a calmer and organized way.

This month, Mercury helps you figure out what you really want. From the 22nd, when it goes into retrograde, it's an excellent time to finish up an unfinished project. Use this time to narrow your attention to the things you enjoy or that allow you to make the most of your abilities. Mars in Cancer is the only shadow on the board, and it will try to get you off track. How? By using your emotions as a guide!

Love

Taurus' energies foster a sense of security in your romantic relationships. It's beautiful that they give you a positive outlook on life. This month, try to enjoy the good things about being romantic. This will keep you from being let down by things you don't really need.

Your union gets back to its normal speed. Everything about it is perfect for you. However, it's possible that your partner will become tired of you after a while. Take a few distracting steps every now and then to avoid problems.

Single Capricorn, Although you may be surprised and seduced by an encounter, this should not be an excuse for succumbing to the siren's song. Instead, stick to your habits and meet more people. After that, you can get to work.

Career

You're still having a hard time with your regular tasks. Achieving your goals requires making concessions and finding solutions. As a result, you're starting to feel a little worn out. All of a sudden, you find yourself running out of patience. If you're a Capricorn, take a walk outside around the 6th of the month and breathe some fresh air. By doing this, you can avoid starting a fight that will be difficult to resolve and, as a side effect, make your life even more unpleasant.

This is a good month for your career, with lots of opportunities for advancement. Most importantly, you have a decent possibility of realizing the benefits you desire. And it's all done without a lot of effort or difficulty.

In addition, you may be able to expand your life in a meaningful way by interacting with others who are more knowledgeable than you. This would add a much-needed dimension to your overall work. A little bit of travel is also a good idea. Some female coworkers or associates may be able to offer you a valuable favor.

Finance

This sector is doing well financially because you are naturally frugal and a great manager.

On the other hand, the augury from the stars doesn't show much good news for your finances this month. You might work hard to reach your goals but not get anywhere because of a series of unfortunate incidences. On top of that, the environment would not be favorable for expanding operations or starting new businesses.

People who work in the arts, like painters, writers, sculptors, and so on, should be prepared for a tough time. Since things are not going well, it would be best to stay out of sight until the bad spell is over.

Health

The way the stars are aligned this month is a clear blessing for your health. In this case, you have nothing to worry about. In fact, your body will get the most out of the food you eat, putting you in the best shape possible. This would mean having a healthy body and mind. You would be able to keep moving and doing things.

Any kind of infection in the chest or lungs must be treated immediately. If this is done, there is no danger or reason to worry. If you didn't do this, your problems would get much worse. The tiniest of details should not be overlooked this month.

Travel

During this month, you should try to travel as little as possible, since doing so won't get you what you want and may even make things worse. There are signs that people whose jobs or businesses require them to travel a lot will be let down.

You wouldn't gain much from traveling, and even trips to the best direction, the West, wouldn't help. People who trade with other countries or have any kind of business with other countries may find, much to their dismay, that their trips abroad turn out to be useless.

Insight from the stars

People play tricks on you by playing on your emotions to get you to give in. Take the lead this time. How? By putting money away at the right time. You will have a lot of opportunities in life, but you should only take the ones that will help you reach your fullest potential.

May 2023

Horoscope

The wild energies of Aries are getting less powerful. On the other hand, those who come from Taurus get their strength back. All of this is proven true on the 17th, when Jupiter moves into Taurus, signaling the return of peace.

Even if you still have to deal with Cancer's energies, the dawning of a new day brightens your day. As a result, you're more likely to participate in the discussion. You've got a lot more patience than you used to! Your decisions are based on what makes sense. The opportunities that present themselves are no longer a source of anxiety and frustration! The risks that were expected to happen don't happen. This month, what Jupiter in Taurus gives you is in line with your values and principles. If you agree, that's fine.

Love

Your affection for your loved ones grows even though you aren't always able to give them your full attention. As a result, you'll feel better when interacting with people or your partner. Concentrate on the positive attributes if you want to make progress.

Things are getting better. As a result, you feel better and better. This month, you will probably spend more time with your partner. If you want the agreement to stay in place, give compliments instead of suggestions.

Single Capricorn, Love returns to a more regular pattern after a period of uncertainty. The meetings and exchanges are becoming increasingly frequent as well. If you want a long-term relationship, you shouldn't focus on the things that irritate you.

Career

Even though this sector is still stressful, it can be dealt with. As stress levels drop, people become less impatient. You find your place. Starting on the 17th, the ideas become concrete proposals. If someone gives you something, Capricorn, tell yourself this is your opportunity. If you do this, you will grow in a universe that is right for you.

A month in which your work is pretty good. There is a good chance that you will achieve the goals you set for yourself, but it would take a lot of hard work. Some of your plans may also involve a certain amount of risk. But since this is a good month, there is almost no chance that something terrible will happen.

Still, it's best not to take chances. The expected gains will not come from travel. There would be a lot of fighting and scheming at work. Also, one of your female coworkers or friends would do you a big favor that would help you greatly.

Finance

When it comes to money, your income could change at the end of the month. You can do what makes you happy all of a sudden.

This month, nothing good will happen to help you financially. This month will be hard for people working with other countries or groups from different states. In fact, they may find themselves working hard to achieve their goals, which may still elude them despite all their hard work.

Also, the climate would not be an excellent place to invest or start a new business. So, if you have plans like this, you should put them off until later. Partnerships and groups of professionals can also cause trouble. Keep your head down until the bad spell is over.

Health

A great month when the stars are aligned to give you good health. You will not only stay healthy, but you will also look great because your body is getting the most out of what you eat. This is the way things should be in a good month.

You are physically, emotionally, and mentally happy all month long. You are always busy and full of energy. The stars want you to be happy throughout this month.

Travel

A month when you won't make much money from traveling because the stars are all against you getting this blessing. Even more so, if you have to travel a lot for business or official work this month, you might not have much to show for your travels at the end of the month.

Even if things were normal, business travel wouldn't be as profitable as it would be in a typical month. Even going in the best direction, the South, wouldn't have the usual effect. Artists, writers, singers, and people like them would find their travels mostly empty and unproductive.

Insight from the stars

This month, be happy and give compliments. This will help your relationships because people will live up to what you expect of them. Work hard to make sure you get what you want. You shouldn't allow yourself to be lazy.

June 2023

Horoscope

The harmonious connection between Jupiter and Saturn shows that your growth is in progress. You can start to work on your goals beginning this month. If you have ideas, now is the time to make sure they come true. The link between Jupiter and Saturn fits with the way you do things. So, take your time, and no one will blame you! Your hard work and willingness to keep going will now be seen and appreciated.

Everything is going well until the 11th. Then, look at what's happening and ask yourself if you're being too hard on others or the situation. If so, you can try to change your strategy by being more friendly and spontaneous.

Love

Venus in Cancer puts you under stress until the 5th. Then you can make up for your absences, unavailability, and mood swings and get back on track. How? Give your loved ones gifts and make big love declarations under the stars.

Between the 5th and the 27th, you have a free field where you can relight the flame. It doesn't really matter what the costs are because the goal has been met; what matters is that it was accomplished!

Single Capricorn Venus doesn't have much of an effect on you this month. So, you will meet a person, but not just anyone. This shows that you can do great things when you're not in a hurry.

Career

Even though you have too much to do, you are like a fish in water. Your patience is awesome, you have great ideas, and you're very good at being everywhere at once. You get right to the point in these situations. Because of this, it can make you a demanding person who expects a lot from other people. Capricorn, ignore what they say if you hear people talking about you behind your back. Your friends and colleagues will be thankful for what you do.

If things go your way, you should do well with your problems over the next month. You would get the expected benefits and wouldn't even have to work hard or do anything out of the ordinary. Also, there wouldn't be any stress at work, making it fun to go to work.

Some female coworker or friend would do you a big favor that would be very helpful. There would also be some travel, which would also be very helpful. Overall, a good month during which you could make a lot of progress.

Finance

From a financial point of view, this is a good time for growth, so grab the ball. You will be glad you did it.

The stars have nothing outstanding to say about your money situation this month. Almost every dispute or lawsuit you might be involved in would go against you. Try to get a decision put off until a later, better time.

People who do business with the government would have to go through a tough phase, as would those who do business with other countries or between states. In short, you would have to work hard and struggle to achieve your planned goals, and even if you did everything right, you wouldn't make much progress. Banks and financial institutions aren't likely to approve loan requests that are still being processed or steps taken to get new loans.

Health

This is a lucky month for your health, as the stars will look out for you. You'd not only feel great, but you'd also look great since your body would be getting the nutrition it needs from your food to the fullest.

A happier emotional and mental state would allow you to live a far more fulfilling and rewarding life. Fortunately, if caught early enough, eye infections can be easily treated, and your month won't be ruined.

Travel

During this month, you won't be able to get the usual benefits from traveling because the stars don't look good. If your job or business requires you to travel a lot, this may not amount to much this month.

Even if you didn't have to work, most travel during this time wouldn't be enjoyable or bring you any significant gains. In some situations, it could even make things worse. This would be true even if you traveled in the best direction, North. If you went on a business trip abroad, you would add a lot to your losses.

Insight from the stars

You need to take a break this month. So, it makes sense that you might want to let go! Do it, and you won't be sorry! To make progress, you must avoid procrastination. Make efficient use of your time. Try new things and push yourself to the limit at the same time.

July 2023

Horoscope

Taurus and Pisces energies allow you to progress at your speed. You take advantage of any opportunity that comes your way, but you do so with the attention to detail that is your trademark. As a result, you are progressing as planned. When Mars moves into Virgo, things take on an entirely new meaning and perspective.

From the 11th on, you have the chance to push the limits of what is possible. You can put your skills and talents to good use if you want to. You will meet people who can push you to grow. Cancer's dissonances will continue to affect you until the 23rd. You may get rid of annoyances by remaining cool in every situation.

Love

Venus wants you to pay attention to the tiniest details, which are actually extremely significant. Get out of your legendary reserve if you want your loves to wake up. Don't be afraid to flaunt your success. Also, don't be surprised if something unexpected happens. Give in gracefully.

Cancer's dissonances are still shaking up your relationship. There are two ways to calm things down. Either you break your piggy bank or do something that will go down in history and give your partner peace of mind for decades.

Single Capricorn, This month, things happen that force you out of your habits and into a new world. You'll meet someone who will put you under their spell. For the next step, believe in yourself. You will be glad you did it.

Career

As of the 11th, your growth is on the right track. The same is true if you wait for a problem to be solved or for ease to come. When Mars is in Virgo, it brings out the best in you. Your plan works out. You know what to do and when to do it. When you need something, you push the limits of what is possible, and it helps you a lot.

This month, your professional prospects are pretty good. You would get the expected benefits, but you might have to do a lot more work. But work would become more enjoyable because the atmosphere would be calm and free of tension.

Some of the women you work with or know would be very helpful and do you a big favor. This would help your chances of getting a job. Expect to do a lot of traveling that pays off. In general, it is a good month.

Finance

On the financial side, unusual circumstances require more resources. You can listen to your heart, but you should also consider what makes sense. If you don't, you might make a choice that costs you more than you thought.

An unlucky month for your finances, according to the stars. Writers, painters, sculptors, and other creative types should prepare for a time of tremendous financial hardship because that might happen.

Even if you were friends with some smart people, you would find it hard to achieve your goals, and even if you did, you wouldn't be very successful. Any pending loan request or plan to get a new loan from banks or other financial institutions is unlikely to be approved. Plans for expansion or starting a new business should be put on hold for now since the time isn't favorable for them.

Health

Thanks to the blessings of the stars, this is a fantastic month for your health. People prone to long-term conditions like rheumatism and complaints like too much gas in the digestive tract will feel much better. The body will be able to fully utilize the nutrients and make effective use of the food eaten for nourishment.

There is a wealth of possibilities for you to live a more fulfilling and rewarding life. Not only in better shape physically but also in a much happier state of mind and heart.

Travel

The stars are not aligned in a way that makes this a good month for travel. Artists, actors, poets, and others in the same line of work would find that their trips to do their jobs don't lead anywhere.

As a result, those who have to travel frequently for work or business may find that their performance falls far short of expectations. This may be especially difficult for sales and marketing professionals. There are also signs that a trip to another country during this time would be just as useless. The best direction would be to go South.

Insight from the stars

The change you've been hoping for is about to happen. To meet it, you should get dressed up and agree to leave your world. Get over the past mistakes. Do not let them define your life.

August 2023

Horoscope

You keep getting better in a world that works for you. Jupiter's Providence provides you with gifts that improve your life. Uranus brings a little bit of the unexpected into your life without making it too unstable. Saturn, on the other hand, gives you plenty of time to get things done.

Everything is fine and getting better. If you'd like to go even further this month, you can do so. Mars and Mercury in Virgo draw attention to how serious you are and how responsible you feel. People who can help you grow will pay attention to you because of who you are. You can talk to them until the 31st. However, if you need to make a decision, you should do it before the 27th because Mars enters Libra on the 28th, making things more complicated.

Love

Venus doesn't have a significant effect on you, but it does have some impact. This month, she makes things worse. Don't take them as signs that love will let you down. Venus makes you aware of something that is meant to push you to make a choice.

There are no conflicts planned. Nothing is wrong. On the other hand, you can get closer to your other half if you want to. How? By spending a few days somewhere else or doing something out of the ordinary.

Single Capricorn, Your dream could come true if you meet that special someone. How? By agreeing to go to a place or area you don't know much about. Or by doing something you like, like a sport or activity.

Career

Capricorn, if you want to go further, you should think about what you suggested a few days or weeks ago. Use this time to carefully read a contract or learn more about something that interests you. Don't forget to think about what you like. You will get what you want if you do this. The expected changes will work out well for you.

Your job prospects are pretty good this month. You might be able to expect to make money, but you would have to work much harder than usual to do so. You could also improve your chances by going on short trips. The workplace atmosphere would also be very friendly, with no sign of trouble. This would make work fun, which would make you happy.

Also, there's a good chance that one of your female friends or coworkers will do you a big favor that will help your career. Overall, this month should be pleasant and helpful, full of accomplishments.

Finance

On the financial side, if a project is delayed, look at it as a good thing and use the time to think about whether you still want to be in this business.

According to the stars, there isn't much good news about your money this month. People who do business between states and other countries would have to deal with challenging conditions. In fact, you would have to work very hard to get the results you want, and even then, you might not get very far.

It wouldn't be a good time to invest or start new businesses. These will probably get stuck. Also, there wouldn't be much chance that banks or other financial institutions would approve any loan applications already in the works. This is not a good time for you, so staying out of the spotlight might be best until the bad time is over.

Health

The stars are shining brightly on your health this month, so take advantage. Your body and mind would benefit significantly from a diet rich in vitamins and minerals, as your system would utilize them to their maximum potential.

There are a few reasons to avoid overworking yourself. As long as it doesn't put too much strain on your body, a reasonable timetable should suffice. A positive outlook and feeling upbeat would keep you physically active and energized throughout the month.

Travel

During this month, the wisest of you can drastically cut back on your travel plans to avoid the adverse effects of the stars, which will keep you from making any significant money through travel. People who have to travel a lot for work or business may be the ones who suffer the most.

But it's comforting to know that these things will lead to better times. Artists, singers, dancers, and others like them may not get the usual benefits from their travels, either. Exporters and others who work with countries outside of the U.S. should also try to avoid going abroad as much as possible since they might not get much out of it.

Insight from the stars

You'd rather do things slowly. But if you want things to change, the time is now. So take your chance and go! Because the future looks promising, you should keep moving forward in your chosen direction.

September 2023

Horoscope

You keep getting better in an environment that helps you grow. When Mercury is in Virgo, you can look at things and plans in great detail. Your thoughts are alive and are working at full speed. You are extremely efficient. As usual, you put your work first. So far, you have not had any particular problems.

Unfortunately, with Mars in Libra, you might have some problems if you don't move on. This month is the time to sync your personal and professional lives. Why? So you don't end up in a bad situation or make a choice you'll later regret. Mars tells you to think about other people if you don't want to be blamed.

Love

Venus still has a tiny effect on the people you care about. Some bad things may happen and catch you by surprise. This month, how your love life goes depends on how well you can find a middle ground. Everything will be fine if you can get your personal life and your work life to work together.

For a while, everything is fine. But the same problems can pop up out of nowhere and cause you and your partner to fight again. But you can avoid it. How? By being there for your partner often and with warmth.

Single Capricorn, You have a good chance of connecting with someone. There is, however, a catch! This month, don't say you're too busy to go out because you have too much work.

Career

This month, a big step will be taken in this field. The bad news is that this good news could be stifled by those who disagree with your goals and ideas. Capricorn, you are a natural star because you are strong and practical. This month, these traits won't help you at all. So, when dealing with specific individuals, use tact and say what they want to hear if you have to. As a result, you'll make rapid progress toward your objectives.

A month with mostly good energy that will help you achieve your professional goals. You may be able to look forward to a lot of travel, which would be very helpful. There is also a good chance that you could make a lot of money from a favor done for you by a female coworker or friend.

A lot of work would be required, but it would be enjoyable due to the positive work environment. But there are reasons to think that some of you might be tempted to break the rules to make quick money. If you gave in to such a temptation, you would never get out of trouble. So, don't do things like that and make the most of a good situation.

Finance

If you're looking to make a big purchase, you'll be able to do it when Venus' retrograde period ends on the 16th.

Your financial future doesn't look very good based on what the stars tell you. Those involved in international trade would be disadvantaged and may have to deal with some difficulties. In fact, you would have to work quite hard to reach your goals, and even then, you probably wouldn't do very well.

In addition, the business climate would remain unfavorable for new businesses and investments. They might get stuck. And finally, any request for a loan or new money from a bank or other financial institution wouldn't have a good chance of being approved.

Health

A great month during which luck is on your side, and you don't have to worry too much about your health. In fact, you can look forward to a period of good luck during which your body will be able to get the most out of the food you eat, absorbing the nutrients and giving your body extra strength and vitality.

You can really look forward to enjoying life and living it more fully and richly. A fun month to look forward to, during which you can stay healthy and have a lot of fun just by not doing anything stupid.

Travel

According to the stars, this month is not a good time to travel. Not only would it not be profitable, but it could even cost you money. On your trips, at least a few of you could get hurt or have some other kind of physical trouble. This is especially true for those of you who like to take risks and try new things.

Even if nothing else went wrong, the trips taken during the month would not have the effect that was hoped for. Even trips to the South, which is the best direction, would be the same. The same thing will happen on trips abroad. In fact, because these things are expensive, they can sometimes make your losses much worse.

Insight from the stars

On the contrary, Mars does not make you miserable. It serves as a reminder of what went wrong in the past so that you don't repeat it. Listen to your intuition and follow your instincts. You can never go wrong if you follow your intuition, no matter what most people think.

October 2023

Horoscope

The dissonances from the planets in Libra force you to live by their rules. When you negotiate, you find a middle ground. You do your best to make yourself more available. Your fans will be sad to find out that this wonderful time will not last.

The transit of Mars into Scorpio on the 13th encourages you to assume leadership responsibilities. It makes you live your life based on your values. This position, which is a bit extreme, may irritate people with soft hearts. So, if you don't want to let criticism get to you, be a little more flexible in dealing with other people, your crew, your fans, or your spouse.

Mercury in Scorpio, which starts on the 23rd, makes you want to lay your cards on the table, but most importantly, do so in a graceful manner.

Love

You may have gone off the rails. Venus in Virgo helps you figure out what you believe in. Despite the pressures and criticism, you continue to pursue your ideals with your loved ones in hand. The mission is done brilliantly by the end of the month.

You prioritize achieving your goals and initiatives above all else. In other words, you're not available to your partner. Unfortunately, this way of life leads to criticism, which you can ease by making a few changes.

Single Capricorn, You have a chance of meeting the right person. Make an effort to be available if you want to build a relationship that will last. Give them time, and don't put them off because you have other things to do.

Career

Libra's dissonances keep pushing you to be more nuanced in your approach. Sometimes you have to work with gullible people who don't know anything about business. On the 13th, the sky starts to clear up. You can make more radical decisions. But be sure to warn the people who need to know and don't put them before the facts. If you don't like this, you should wait until the 23rd.

A pretty good month for your career to get the expected benefits, but you would also have to work very hard. But doing hard work in a great workplace makes it fun, which is what you can expect.

There is a good chance that a female coworker or associate will do you a big favor that will help your career in a big way. This would really help you. Those who work in the pure sciences and medicine may be able to expect to do incredibly well. Traveling, on the other hand, would be highly beneficial.

Finance

From the 9th, you become more reasonable when it comes to money. You have a keen eye for detail when managing your assets. If you're hoping for a positive response at the end of the month, you'll receive one.

A good month for your finances, during which you could make a lot of money, but not without any problems. The success of your projects, no matter what they are, would be boosted by your friendships with smart, spiritually-minded people. In fact, this would add a delightful layer of culture and sophistication to your entire working life.

You'd be able to achieve most of your goals and make the most money from them. Still, you'll likely run into problems along the way. There is also a chance of being late for an important meeting. But success is sure to happen. A good time to not only get a lot done but also to feel a lot of satisfaction.

Health

A month in which your health has been blessed by the stars and you have little to be concerned about. As a result, your system will not only be healthy but also look healthy, and you'll be a lot more energetic and active.

Only one thing could go wrong: an accident or a violent, serious injury, so extreme caution is advised. This, though, is a remote possibility.

Always keep an eye on your health. You may uncover long-term health issues this early in your life. Rest, a good diet, avoiding stressful circumstances, and bottled-up emotions can all help keep things from getting worse. Storing up destructive emotions can lead to the development of a hidden sickness, which can then lead to other problems.

Travel

The stars don't look good for you this month when it comes to travel, so don't count on going anywhere. Artists, singers, dancers, actors, and people like them would not be able to make any money during their stays.

Most of you fit this description. The stars predict sales and marketing workers will be the hardest hit. They may not be able to meet the goals set out in the contract. Traveling also wouldn't be all that enjoyable and there may also not be the usual second chance. People who want to go abroad to get a higher education may face different problems. This month, the best direction to travel is North.

Insight from the stars

You've regained control of your life, which is a good thing. Using firmness, however, will do you no good; instead, use tact and diplomacy. You must be on the lookout for potential threats to your well-being. If you make a single mistake, your overall health could be in jeopardy.

November 2023

Horoscope

You are surrounded by planetary forces that stimulate and support your growth. You're shielded from danger by a force you can't put your finger on. With an approach that is uniquely yours, you suddenly make significant progress toward your goal. You're determined to alter the direction of events with Mars in Scorpio till the 24th. Despite the positive atmosphere, there is a glimmer of doubt on the blackboard.

When Venus is in Libra from the 9th to the 30th, its dissonances tell you that there will be tensions that you will have to ease. Your personal growth has accelerated considerably in the past month. If you want things to go well, be sure to tell your friends and family what you plan to do. Why? for the simple reason that they are terrified of change.

Love

Everything is fine until the 8th. Then there's Venus in Libra, which brings the problems back. Things can grow frustrating if you can't keep the attention of your significant other or your followers. Be soothing in order to avoid criticism. It's small, but it'll spare you a lot of hassle down the road.

Things are back to normal now. Sadly, this happiness won't last long. When Venus moves through Libra, your partner is more likely to be in a mood that irritates you. Keep your cool, and everything will work out.

Single Capricorn, Getting someone to like you is a piece of cake. Sadly, this good fortune might be broken if you don't do what's right. Give someone you've met sometime this month, even if your time is valuable.

Career

You are doing great this month, and the right people come into your life at the right time. Your decisions are sound. Customers and employees are drawn to you because of your charisma. Under these conditions, you are sure to make progress. You seem too good at getting what you want. However, all of this can be stopped by people who aren't as brave as you, Capricorn. Take the time to tell them how you will do it. This will give them peace of mind.

This month, you would have great opportunities to move up in your career, but you would also have more work to do. You may be looking forward to getting what you expect. There would be no stress in the workplace, and everyone would enjoy coming to work.

In addition, a female coworker or associate may be able to help you advance your career. This should have a significant impact. In addition to that, traveling would be a great way to make money. In this situation, you would also get a lot of pleasure from your work, which would give you a sense of accomplishment. Overall, this is a good month for you, and you should do well at work.

Finance

Financially, this industry is booming because, by its very nature, no one throws their money away. As a result, the necessities of daily life are well covered, as is leisure time.

This month, your financial situation looks pretty good. There is a good chance that an old friend could do you a big favor that would help you greatly. You could expect more good luck if you worked with someone of the female sex in a business partnership or partnership. This could also make a lot of money.

It would be an excellent time to start new businesses and invest. And those of you who have similar plans should get them moving. Also, there would be a good chance that banks and other financial institutions would approve any loan requests already in the works or any new proposals for new loans.

Health

This is an excellent month for your health. The stars are aligned in your favor, so you don't have much to worry about. People prone to long-term conditions like rheumatism and digestive tract problems will feel better.

When your body absorbs all the nutrients from the food you eat, you will feel good about your health and look good. Not only will you be very active and full of energy, but your mind will also be in good shape. A nice month that would require you to do very little work.

Travel

According to the stars, this is a good month to travel. Those whose jobs or businesses require a lot of travel may be in an enviable position, with things going as planned and meeting your expectations.

People in sales and marketing would do well if they went in the most favorable direction, which is South, as it would lead to the expected result. Also, there is a good chance that business trips outside the country will live up to expectations.

Insight from the stars

Even though it's not who you are, try to be comforting to other people. This won't change how your life goes, but it will keep you from dealing with things you don't need to. Because business is booming and you're making more money than you expected, you're going to expand your operation.

December 2023

Horoscope

Luck is constantly on your side, and you plan to take advantage of it. However, the pace is less steady than it was last month.

This month, your progress is helped by Mercury in Capricorn from the 2nd to the 23rd and by Venus in Scorpio from the 5th to the 29th. Because of these planetary energies, it's no longer a good idea to make decisions based just on your judgment but rather to persuade your coworkers or partners. Mercury helps you build your personality so that you can do well with this little trick. He is connected to Venus and tells you to strengthen the bonds that link you to the people who can help you.

You finish the year without major issues. However, if you have periods of inaction, do not become alarmed. Seize the moment to do a self-evaluation.

Love

Until the 4th, you have to put in some work. Then, with Venus in Scorpio, you go through a time of ease, which you love. This month, you are back in complete charge of the situation. People know they can count on you and your loyalty without you doing anything special.

It's time for your relationship to get back to cruise speed after a period of ups and downs. As a result, it's time to revisit the projects that were put on hold. Why? Because it'll provide your spouse a lot of comfort for years to come.

Single Capricorns, You could meet your soulmate. You don't have to do anything at all to succeed at this little wonder. And if you want to, you can even talk to them about your latest business plan! This special someone will be enchanted!

Career

Now is not the time to make a decision about anything. Instead, think about the work that has been done in recent times. Capricorn, even though you are very focused, take short breaks. Why? Because some files need to be worked on. People need to know what happened after an event. A project needs your attention to keep going until next year.

According to the horoscope, the stars don't see much hope for your career this month. With much more work to do, you would put in a lot of effort for what would definitely not be enough payoff. The situation would be made better in some ways by a pleasant and stress-free work environment. But only so much and not more.

Travel would likewise fall short of your expectations, yet a trip to the South might provide some benefits. Not enough to make up for the whole thing, it must be said. Contacts won't be very helpful, making a difficult situation even harder. Also, don't do anything illegal, which could worsen your problems.

Finance

You'll go over your budget if you wait until the last minute to make your holiday purchases. So, plan ahead of time instead of dwelling on something that will occur on the 24th.

Because the stars are favorably aligned, this month has good financial prospects. There is a good probability that an old friend could help you out in a big way. Some of you would also be lucky that a partnership or a professional relationship with a woman would be beneficial.

You would also know how to handle your employees or subordinates in a way that lets you get the most out of their work. This would be a big win. The climate would also be good for investing or starting new businesses, so those with such plans should go ahead and implement them.

Health

A month in which the stars are very kind to your health, and you have nothing to worry about. Your body would get the most out of the food you eat, which could show in your glowing health.

Not only will you be very active throughout the month, but you'll also be in such good shape that life will be much richer and fuller in every way. There is a chance of overworking. But you can get past this with a smartly planned schedule that doesn't stress you. Overall, it's a good month that lets you enjoy life.

Travel

The stars are in your favor this month, so you may expect to reap substantial rewards from your travels. Most of you would be able to accomplish your goals with ease if you had to travel frequently for work. Travel options include flying, taking a train, or driving. The South is the most favorable direction.

Some of you may also be able to make a profitable business trip abroad for international travel. You would also have a nice vacation.

Insight from the stars

Everything is going well this month. Be prepared for brief moments of inaction, however. They're designed to get you thinking about how you might improve your plan. Be wary of bargains that seem too good to be true. During the Mercury retrograde period of 2023, avoid making any speculative investments you are unsure about.